The Hall Closet

by Jane Web
illustrated by Meryl Henderson

Practice Decodable 45

Mc Graw Hill Education

Bothell, WA • Chicago, IL • Columbus, OH • New York, NY

MHEonline.com

Send all inquiries to:
McGraw-Hill Education
8787 Orion Place
Columbus, OH 43240

ISBN: 978-0-02-133282-3
MHID: 0-02-133282-7

Printed in the United States of America.

7 8 9 CTM 23

"Mom! Six big things are in the hall closet!"

"They have black ribbons and no hands!"

"Did they dig a path to the hall closet?"

"Will they get out if they have banana snacks?"

“Can I get the big things out of the closet?”

"It is just Anna! Get to bed, Anna."